Designing Interiors with **tile**

ROCKPORT

Designing Interiors with **tile**

GLOUCESTER MASSACHUSETTS

ROCKPORT PUBLISHERS

CREATIVE IDEAS WITH

CERAMIC, STONE, AND MOSAIC

ANNA KASABIAN

with **JULIE GOODMAN**

First published in the United States of America by
Rockport Publishers, Inc.
33 Commercial Street
Gloucester, Massachusetts 01930-5089
Telephone: (978) 282-9590
Facsimile: (978) 283-2742
www.rockpub.com

ISBN 1-56496-580-5

10 9 8 7 6 5 4 3 2 1

Printed in China

FRONT COVER IMAGES (CLOCKWISE FROM TOP LEFT):
TILE: Ann Sacks Tile and Stone; DESIGN: Beverly Hammel, Rutt of
Chicago. TILE: Bisazza.TILE: Pewabic Tile; DESIGN: Rosemary Porto
Interiors; PHOTO: Stephen Sette-Ducati. TILE: Waterworks. TILE:
Bisazza. DESIGN: Michael R. Golden Design.

BACK COVER IMAGE:
Tile: Pratt and Larson.

IMAGES ON PAGE 8 (CLOCKWISE FROM TOP RIGHT):
TILE: Ann Sacks Tile and Stone; DESIGN: Beverly Hammel, Rutt of
Chicago. TILE: Fired Earth.TILE: Artistic Tile. TILE: Waterworks.
TILE: Pratt and Larson; PHOTO: Jon Jensen.

IMAGE ON PAGES 14 AND 15:
TILE: Vidrepur, Spain; Photo: Spanish Ceramic Tile Manufacturers
Association (ASCER).

IMAGES ON PAGE 16 (CLOCKWISE FROM TOP LEFT):
TILE: Ann Sacks Tile and Stone; DESIGN: Marci Feigen; PHOTO:
Peter Ledwith. TILE: Cerabec, Spain. DESIGN: Todd Oldham;
PHOTO: Todd Eberle; LOCATION: The Hotel, Miami, Beach, Florida.
TILE: Bisazza.

IMAGES ON PAGES 38 AND 39:
DESIGN: Michael R. Golden Design.

IMAGE ON PAGE 40:
TOP LEFT: TILE: Michael R. Golden Design.

IMAGES ON PAGE 62 (CLOCKWISE FROM TOP LEFT):
TILE: Ann Sacks Tile and Stone. ARCHITECT: Bershad Design Associates,
Inc.; CONTRACTOR: PM Dandini Construction; PHOTO: Eric Roth.
DESIGN: Arthur de Mattos Casas; PHOTO: Tuva Reines.
TILE: Molais Roman Mosaic, Itlay.

IMAGE ON PAGE 84:
DESIGN: Arthur de Mattos Casas.

IMAGE ON PAGE 85:
TILE: Walker Zanger; Design: Center Q Designs, Susan Whitman; PHOTO:
Stuart Watson.

IMAGE ON PAGE 108:
BOTTOM LEFT: TILE: Artistic Tile.

IMAGE ON PAGES 126 AND 127:
TILE: WC Tile Guild/Country Floors; DESIGN: Mitch Chester ASID/Jamie
Gibbs and Associates; PHOTO: Oleg March.

IMAGES ON PAGE 128 (CLOCKWISE FROM TOP LEFT):
TILE: Italy. TILE: Pratt and Larson; PHOTO: Jon Jensen.
TILE: Fired Earth. TILE: Oceanside Glasstile, Inc./ Tiles,
A Refined Selection.

BOOK DESIGN: Mimi Ahmed, Stephen Perfetto, Leeann Leftwich.

ACKNOWLEDGMENTS

My thanks, first, to all the interior designers, architects, photographers, tile designers, and manufacturers for their cooperation and contributions. They made this book happen, and it is their work that will inspire. Special thanks to Ann Sacks for her time and generosity.

At Rockport, my sincere thanks to Shawna Mullen for introducing me to this wonderful book, and to my editor, Martha Wetherill. She, no matter what, was always calm, attentive, fair, and a pleasure to work with.

Dedicated to my husband, David, whose positive energy and support were constant.   Anna Kasabian

Contents

W hen I was a young girl, my introduction to stone, tile, mosaic, and marble was in public places. The marble columns of my church were grand and begged my little hand to run over them or to gently follow a colorful pattern. The auditory feedback was amusing, and it always felt so cool to the touch! Later, in my travels to Italy, Switzerland, London, Mexico, and the Caribbean, I saw amazing works of art composed of these materials. Seeing how artisans have crafted interiors and exteriors with these materials is food for our souls and imaginations.

Today, introducing these materials into homes and land-scapes is very popular. Trend-watchers like Faith Popcorn comment that the chaos of the world makes people cocoon in their homes. They are feathering their nests, turning up the volume on comfort and luxury. Baths have become tiled spas, bedrooms full of down comforters, pillows, and all things cozy. Fireplaces,

always a focal point, are in vogue and, because of that, stone and tile are getting special attention. People spend more time in kitchens, thanks to Martha Stewart and others who champion the virtues of stirring pots of hearty soup. So kitchens, too, are being eyed for beautiful tile and stone, with stoves as centerpieces.

People are demonstrating a renewed appreciation for craftsmanship and objects that express history, so tile and stone that appear old are in demand. Decorating with these materials adds to a sense of comfort and allows the homeowner's individuality to shine through.

In reviewing this collection of rooms, patios, solariums, and poolside areas, make note of the stone, marble, mosaics or color palettes and patterns that appeal to you. With your designer, architect, or tile installer, create rooms with new views.

Anna Kasabian

When you enter the world of tile and stone, it is not long before you hear the name Ann Sacks. Her line of tile and stone, comprising hundreds of patterns, palettes, and textures, is artistic and functional. She prides herself on overseeing the development of new designs and finding special small digs that unearth the most unusual stone.

Between 1981 and 1987, Ms. Sacks opened three showrooms in the United States, and within two years her company joined the Kohler family of businesses. Today she has showrooms across the country; more than thirty dealers and more than thirty artists work exclusively for her. She continues to import tile and stone from around the world and is always looking for unique tile that she can add to her line.

Have you seen renewed interest in tile and stone?

It's been growing dramatically over the past few years. The market has gone from pragmatic to both sophisticated and practical. A third of what we sell is imported from Europe, actual antique materials like old terra-cotta and old limestone, and we have some proprietary programs that are the result of our going to small quarries. Painted tile is a small portion of what we do, and we have a few limited hand-painted programs from Europe; Portugal has the best.

How did Ann Sacks Tile and Stone start?

It was in the early 1980s. In Oregon, no tile was available that was warm as opposed to institutional, more about beauty than utility. One day I went into a store to buy a dress and saw some colorful terra-cotta tiles for sale. I thought I could sell more of them if I used them to tile a room. So I did. I put them in my old house and covered my

wood floors with Saltello floor tiles, which was a sin at the time, and covered every room with decorative tiles, even my dining-room table, where I put Talavera tiles. I ran tiny black-and-white ads and began to sell tile out of my house. Later, when I offered to match a discontinued tile color and recruited a local craftsman to reproduce it, my custom colored tile line—the Ann Sacks Collection—was born. That went on to become the most successful tile program in the country.

(above and opposite) Tile: Ann Sacks Tile and Stone

Do tile makers come to you with ideas?

Yes. But the first thing I want to know is how they make the tile and the kind of clay they use. I start from the technology end because then I know what styles can evolve from the technique. If it's hand-painted tile, I'm going to go to England and look at someone who has been trained at the Royal Academy of Art. I've got to take that route because the hand-painted area is the noisiest and least quality-driven segment. Today, artists come to me with a program. If it's technically good and the person is savvy, that is what counts.

Do you favor tile over stone?

I am most connected to stone. I find it the most compelling material in the world. I do love tile, but in general, I think, there are more misses in tile than stone. It can be a disappointing medium if it's mishandled.

When people look through this book, they will get ideas on how to use tile and stone. When they go to a showroom, should they seek out what they love and buy it?

I think it's important for us to advise customers on their choices. The customer is not in a position to visualize what a room full of tile or stone will look like. I don't think we should just let people fall in love. Like a parent, we should help steer the course. You can have a lot of fun in a room, but you need to have a relationship between the room and the tile or stone. Then you need to carry the theme throughout the home. You should not bounce from one theme to another. One thing that we do is continue to edit our tile and stone programs and delete something we see is not working out. I think it's our responsibility to show customers what works well with what, and I tell the salespeople to do the same.

How do you steer people in the right direction?

We ask our customers, "How do you want your house to feel?" And we get answers like warm, comfortable, orderly, light, eclectic. From there, we show tile options that we feel will contribute to that expressed direction and try to relate it all to subsequent selections.

You are in the middle of your own home-design project. Tell us what you are doing with stone and tile.

As I said, you can have fun and, at the same time, you need to carry a theme. I am building an apartment on top of a commercial building we are developing that will be the most modern retail building in Portland. A wall of 14-foot-high glass runs across the front of my apartment. My floor will be covered in 5- by 3-foot slabs of ochre stone to give it a warm but contemporary feeling. My kitchen will be contemporary, with lots of stainless steel, and one bath will be done in gray stone in keeping with the mood of the kitchen. A second bath, also very contemporary, will be done using Israeli mosaic corners, which, when put together to form a square, create a charming, primitive pattern. For the walls of the bath, I am using French terra-cotta that was sanded and looks very earthy.

How do you see tile and stone fitting into today's home?

It's a major element, and I'm seeing it chosen more and more over wood flooring. It's being used in kitchens and dining rooms, entryways, and baths. Tile is being used up the walls, making the whole room feel richer. Vertical use of tile is even more effective than tile floors if you want to impart a European feeling to your home design.

What are some of the new tile and stone colors, patterns, and blends that you see for the year 2000?

I see the interest in modern finishes, which was 100 percent absent in the 1980s, returning a bit in the 1990s. Now there is a real appreciation for modern materials. People are using larger formats, which are more monolithic, and they're using more glass and metal. And this is all softened by the handcrafted work that, while it is modern, is not cold. I like to think, too, that gray is finally here. We are making a decent commitment to it, as well as making things work well with cream.

(opposite) Tile: Ann Sacks Tile and Stone

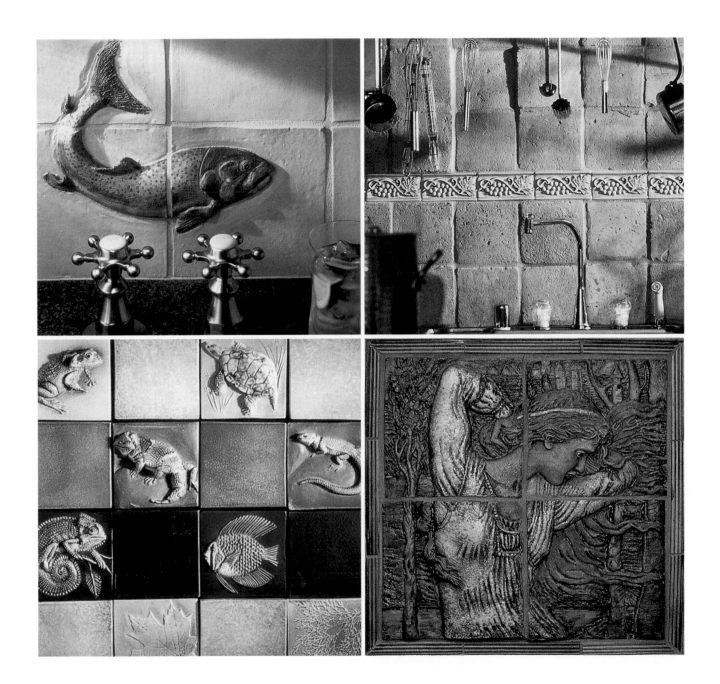

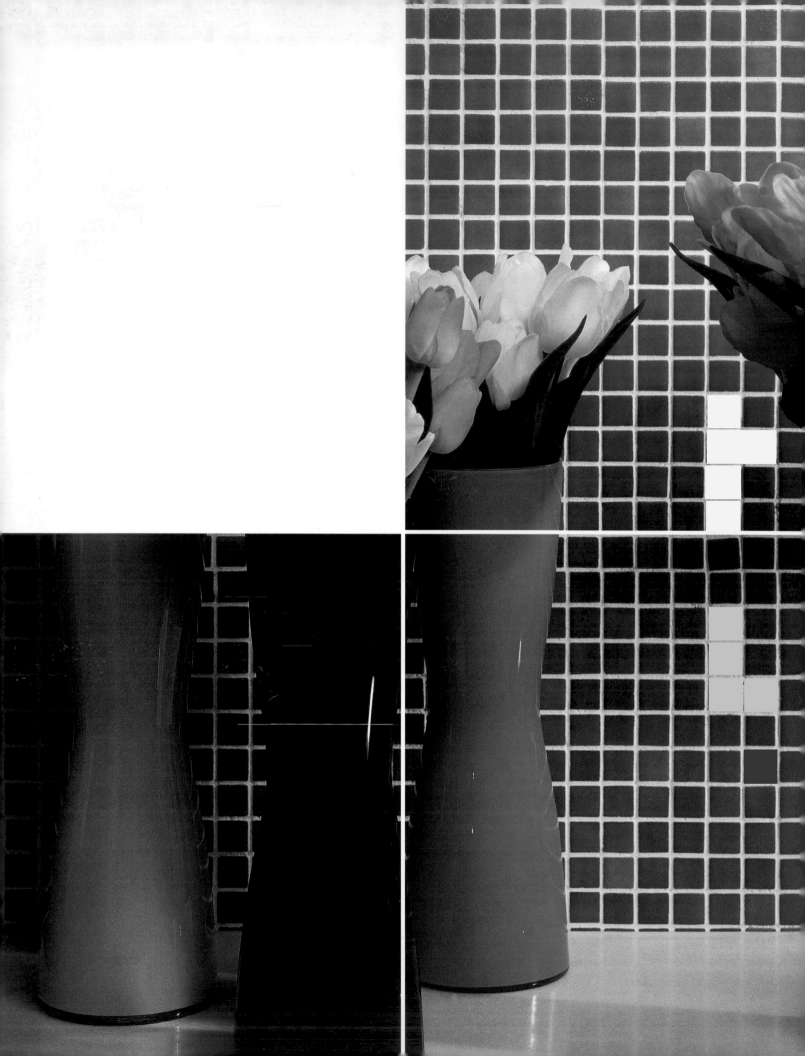

Color

For centuries, ceramic tile makers experimented to broaden the range of colors they could achieve, subjecting different colors of clay and mineral glazes to the alchemy of the kiln. Modern chemistry and production technologies have added new shades as well as new ways of achieving gradations of color within a single tile.

The highest of high-tech methods are applied to imitate the look and touch of ancient handmade tiles. New raw materials have replaced substances such as lead that were used in the past but are today considered environmentally sensitive. Today, manufacturers may subject a tile to more than twenty separate decorating procedures—painting, brushing, spattering—to duplicate the beauty and subtle variations in color and texture produced by the presence of lead in a glaze. From electric brights to soft neutrals, the ever-widening range of tile colors that found favor in the early 1990s is more complex today, enriched by nuanced mixtures and muted midtones. New techniques produce metallic, opalescent, and iridescent finishes, while faux stone is made in all the natural pinks, greens, grays, and golds of marble and granite. The popularity of multicultural influence is reflected in a world of imported ethnic tiles—earthy Mexican terra-cottas, exuberant Portuguese colors, classic Dutch blues and whites, elaborate Moroccan patterns. At the millennium, our attention is turned to the past; historic tiles of every period and style are being reproduced by manufacturers and tile artists alike.

Choosing and using color in interior design can establish a mood, arouse or calm the emotions, and evoke a particular style of living or historic era. This chapter explores the use of color in a variety of rooms, in a variety of distinctive expressions.

(above) Create an intricate multicolored tile rug to liven up an entry-way. Mix ceramic with mosaic in concentric circles and free yourself to accepting the decor possibilities. Tile: Illahe Tileworks; Design and Installation: Susan S. Werschkul; Photo: Patricia Bean. (right) Give a bathroom a cool, back-to-nature texture and mood with garden-green tile walls finished with a leaf border and accenting terra-cotta stone tile floors. Tile: ICT, Inc.; Tile Design: Talavera de Mexico; Interior Design: Susan Baker, Houston; Photo: Jack Thompson; Home: Susannah and David Schorlemer, Houston.

Plan carefully to successfully combine seven kinds of tile and stone. Notice how clusters of colors draw the eye around this bathroom and that some of the small wall tiles sport question marks, circles, or letters—a humorous touch. The tile that caps and finishes the wall catches the attention with shorthand squiggles. Finally, the high-gloss marble floor keeps the room feeling cool and clean. Photo: Stephen Cridland.

(above) Transform a low-light work area into a rainbow of color
with tile. Photo: Tim Street-Porter. (right) For people who need help
waking up in the morning, install a sunrise of tile in an array of
energizing shades. This cheery bath also features a wall of glass tile;
peer through, and the colored tiles take on kaleidoscopic patterns
and shapes. Photo: Tim Street-Porter.

(left) Consider using repeating tile murals as if they were wallpaper. They can brighten a corner in need of color or an entire room, and they can form a rich backdrop for furniture, fabric, and art. Tile: Walker Zanger; Photo: Stuart Watson.

(above) Create a patchwork of art tiles, as the owners of this Houston home did, by piecing together a variety of tradition-al, century-old Spanish Talavera tile patterns rather than building an interlocking pattern or border with just one. Tile: ICT, Inc.; Tile Design: Talavera de Mexico; Interior Design: Susan Baker, Houston; Photo: Jack Thompson; Home: Susannah and David Schorlemer, Houston.

(right and opposite) Set a tranquil mood with a wall of soft moss-green tiles. For a functional, stylish bathroom, add elegant details like frosted glass shelving, accents of silver, and engaging wide-rimmed vessel sinks. Complement blonde woods and simple platform countertops with textural, earth-toned floor tiles. Tiles: Kohler Company; Design: Cynthia Leibrock and Eva Maddox Design.

COLOR

Place tile to provide visual clues to utilitarian functions. In this bathroom, the checkerboard of yellow and white tile leads to the tub. Mixing small tiles with larger ones, and varying their shapes and colors, adds to the room's overall interest. Photo: Stephen Cridland.

Introduce vivid tile colors to your fireplace and create a focal point for a room. This Long Island getaway has color as its theme. Design: Charles Riley; Photo: Philip H. Ennis Photography.

(left) Consider designing your own trompe l'oeil tile rug to add color to a dark kitchen or break up a monochromatic floor. Tile: Tile By Design; Photo: Leonard Myszynski. **(above) You can use color to take you to another time and place. The walls of this powder room were covered in a soft, pink-glazed ceramic tile in order to create a glamorous hideaway—the kind a starlet from the 40s might retreat to for a long bath. The designer of this luxurious room chose this pink tile for its sense of "Old World textural sexiness, and because it's effective at creating a sense of age."** Tile: California Art Tile, Pacific Design Center, Kohler Company; Interior Design: Mark Enos; Photo: David Glomb.

(opposite and above) Italian terra cotta and ceramic tiles in vibrant colors totally energize a room. The design lesson here is that you can use tile to warm up, cool down, or feel as though you're sipping morning tea in Tuscany. Tile: Bardelli, Cerasarda, and Il Pavone, Italy; Tile Design: Michael R.Golden Design; Interior Design: Carol Helms, *Garden Design Magazine*; Photos: Andre Baranowski.

(above) Get wild with tile to show that it can stand alone as art. This colorful, funky bath makes the point perfectly. A wall of air-brushed tile frames the sink and contrasts with the geometric patterns on the floor and in the shower. Interior and Tile Design: Todd Oldham; Photo: Todd Eberle; Hotel: The Hotel, Miami Beach, Florida. (right) Choose a soft green cover of tile for a bath overlooking a flowering garden. The combination of greens, indoors and out, makes for a relaxing atmosphere in which to soak. Interior Design: Frank Fitzpatrick; Photo: Tim Street-Porter.

Mosaics and Murals

Exotic and colorful, mosaics are among the most ancient forms of decoration. Clay mosaics ornamented the walls of Sumerian temples in Mesopotamia five thousand years ago. The great civilizations of the ancient world produced magnificent mosaics, still visible in Egyptian tombs, Roman pavements, and Byzantine churches.

Today, mosaics and murals are experiencing a renewal of popularity as designers rediscover the creative possibilities of the medium. In interiors, mosaics are applied lavishly to decorate entire walls and floors, or used sparingly to enrich monochromatic tiled surfaces with the addition of color accents and elegant borders.

Mosaic designs are made by setting small squares or pieces (tesserae) of tile, stone, glass, or other materials into a background of cement or grout. Mosaics are small, multicolored stones cut into various shapes that, when viewed from a distance, can coalesce into photographic-style portraits or patterns.

Viewed up close, each small tessera is just one square or spot of color and texture. Assembled and blended, they can form shapes, patterns, images, pictures, and words. The repetitive patterning of the tiny mosaic tesserae is hypnotically pleasing to the eye.

The designer working with mosaics uses tesserae with slight differences and variations in color and shape to achieve soft outlines and a uniquely handmade feel. Arranging mosaic tiles according to subtle gradations of color can produce a full tonal range and the illusion of three dimensions.

Creating elaborate mosaic designs is a laborious and meticulous art, but the advent of the computer has made it possible to produce intricate patterns in a fraction of the time it takes to assemble tesserae by hand. Of course, mosaics set by machine cannot duplicate the subtle variations and slight imperfections that make handmade mosaics distinctive and highly prized. They are best used for repetitive designs, such as borders and trims, where precision is desirable. Intricate or simple, geometric or figural, mosaics and murals add color, texture, and dimension to your rooms.

If you have a special vision for your bath, consider plotting out your own tile design. This bathroom, a mix of 4,186 hand-cut tiles and thirteen colors, is just what the owners in Cedar Falls, Iowa, ordered. Tile: Sunny Days Flooring; Design: Robert Cisar.

Convey an elegant look with earth-toned mosaic tiles. In this bathroom, the neutral colors meld into a complex, interesting texture off which light is free to play. Interior Design: Scott Johnson; Photo: Tim Street-Porter.

Enhance both color and a visual theme by adding a repeated mural pattern to tilework. In this bright bath, the flower theme is catalyzed by the purple wisteria that works its way around the room. Interior Design: Sam Botero; Photo: Philip H. Ennis Photography.

(left) There is no need to hang photos in this magnificent, high-detail kitchen. Let colorful mural tiles work their way around your ceiling edge, each within their own wood frame. Around the stovetop, allow repeating patterns to create a stunning storage area for a cluster of copper pans and racked spices. Tile: Country Floors. (below) Introduce decorative tiles to your fireplace and make that an integral part of your design and color theme. Tile: Country Floors.

(right) Mosaics can be the design focal point in a room and set the palette for furnishings. Tile: Artistic Tile. (below) Create an old-world feel with a wall of mosaics and a vessel sink. Tile: Artistic Tile. (opposite) This arts-and-crafts–style border forms a mural that works well with the pedestal sink and metal mirror frame. Tile: Walker Zanger; Photo: Stuart Watson.

(left) Encase a bathroom sink with basketweave mosaic tiles that resemble a soft fabric cover. The small tiles contrast well with the mosaic-bordered mirror and the diamond and square-shaped stones on the walls. Tile: Country Floors. **(above)** Tile: Artistic Tile.

(left) **Study the choices carefully before selecting tile for murals; decide how great a part they should play in the overall design. These beautiful ceramic mural tiles are functional at splash level and provide colorful, engaging scenes that are abstractly repeated in the bottom wall border and on the floor.** Tile: Walker Zanger; Photo: Stuart Watson. **(below) Introduce a new art form in a room with a mix of mosaic and decorative relief stone.** Tile: Country Floors.

(opposite) Consider laying an elegant underwater mosaic carpet for an indoor pool. Cool blue and warm yellow tiles create patterns that work well with natural light. Palace in Riyadh, Saudi Arabia; Design: Erika Brunson Design Associates. (left) Detail a fireplace in colorful mosaic tiles to secure its role as the focal point of a sitting room—with or without the flames. Photo: Tim Street-Porter.

(opposite) Convey an elegant look with earth-toned and cool gray mosaic tiles. In this bathroom, the neutral colors meld into a complex, interesting texture off which light is free to play. Interior Design: Scott Johnson; Photo: Tim Street-Porter. **(above) A windowless powder room is transformed into a Victorian conservatory by latticework, vines, and flowers of glass mosaics, highlighted with eighteen-carat gold chips. A terra-cotta planter for the sink completes this charming indoor garden.** Design: Michael R. Golden Design; Photo: Tim Lee.

(above) Go all out with gorgeous iridescent tiles that look as though they've been shaken off the wings of butterflies. Complete the look with a crystal sink cradled on what appears to be a floating silver tray. This is drama at its best. Tile: Kohler Company. **(right) Line a shower stall with shimmering glass mosaics to create a color extravaganza.** Tile: Bisazza.

Atmosphere and Drama

The saying, "A man's home is his castle," rings true with today's tile, stone, and mosaic options. Any room, or an entire home, can be made to feel like a castle with these materials—or like a Roman bath, or like a French country villa. A first step to designing with tile, stone, or mosaic is to think first about the mood that will be evoked. Other considerations, aside from budget, are the size and function of the room, the availability of natural light, the intensity of foot traffic, and the style of the furnishings. The good news is that there are hundreds and hundreds of choices of materials. The challenge is to select the right ones, as it is inconvenient to remove them if you change your mind.

This chapter shows how architects and designers turn bathrooms into oases of quiet and calm, how mosaics can function as striking rugs of color, and how a rooftop patio can seem miles from the chaos of the city. Use the atmosphere and drama depicted here as inspiration for creative expression on the blank canvas that is your home.

(left) Make everyday bathing a spa experience with white-on-white tiles in an oversized shower. For subtle detailing that transcends the merely clinical, add a mix of mosaic tile on the floor and diamond-shaped tile insets on the walls. Frame the tile in buttercup-yellow woodwork to help it stand out. Photo: Roger Turk/Northlight Photography.

(above) Thoughtfully place skylights to give a wall of tile as many moods as the weather. This architectural glass tile was designed to have a slightly worn, handcrafted quality; no two pieces are alike. In this room, it wraps around the curve of a free-standing wall so that it resembles a huge, surreal wave. Tile: Ann Sacks Tile and Stone.

ATMOSPHERE AND DRAMA

(opposite and left) Base a bathroom design on the Haman or Turkish bath; start with a waxed terra-cotta floor highlighted with a biblical limestone mosaic. Use pigmented concrete—a waterproof surface with an earthy patina—to line a domed open shower. Repeat the pigmented concrete approach for a handcrafted sink. Interior Design: Cachet Interiors, Thomas A. Hays; Photos: Douglas Kilpatrick.

(right) Try hexagonal golden stone tiles to make a sitting room glow. These work nicely to complement the fabric and wall treatment. Tile: Cotto D'este, Italy. (below) Focus attention on a rug of mosaic tile, patterned with leaves and flowers and bordered in a wide band of bone and brown. This sitting room features lemony yellow walls and fabric choices that play off the mosaic color theme. Tile: Ann Sacks Tile and Stone.

(left) Plan every detail when designing a set. Here, the tiles, the tub, the fixtures, the woodwork, and the photographs work together to give the feel of days gone by. Photo: Roger Turk/Northlight Photography. **(right) Plant big, square, sunset-colored stone tiles to give a room a big, open, and airy feeling. The flooring shown here also sets off the deep, rich colors of the furniture and area rug.** Tile: Vives Azulejos, Italy.

Use tile to support a design theme and capture the feeling of another era. Here, an old-fashioned pedestal sink and antique dressing table are complemented by tilework set in a classic pattern with a simple color palette. Photo: Tim Lee.

(above) Separate two kinds of stone tiles with a band of colorful decorative stone to make a sunny terrace feel like two outdoor rooms. Add the accent of warm wood in the furniture and greenery to create a special place to read, dine, or entertain. Tile: Ceramica Saloni, Italy. (right) Create an engaging, dramatic patio environment by mixing and matching tile work from the floor to the walls, and on up the doorways. Here, six-sided terra-cotta floor tiles work well with all of the interestingly shaped planters and sculpture. Colorful ceramic tables complement the decorative wall tiles and tile mural, and the distinctive vertical tile bands around doorways punctuate the drama. Tile: Country Floors.

(left) Scale back the bustle common to most kitchens with a subdued palette. Here, a green concrete tile floor; smooth, silvery surfaces; and frosted-glass closures carry the theme. Interior Design: Cachet Interiors, Thomas A. Hays; Photo: Lynn Massimo. **(above) Complement open architecture and earthy tones with terracotta tiles for a casual, comfortable breakfast room.** Design: Ann Lenox; Photo: Steve Vierra Photography.

(above) Give a bright white bath with an oversized soaking tub a classy and classic look with gold accents. The big, square Spanish tiles lead the way to this high-ceilinged room, and the cap of yellow is a smart touch that makes this a sunny place, rain or shine. Tile: Vives, Spain. (right) Give a narrow, windowless hallway—like the main entrance to this Boston penthouse—an open, stylish feel with a classic-patterned marble floor. The sweep and drama of the space prepare the visitor for a memorable interior. Interior Design: Anthony Catalfano; Photo: Steve Vierra Photography.

(above) Create a distinctly feminine bathroom with the right combination of tile. Here, shades of blush-toned Italian tiles form a wall of diamonds accented at the tub and ceiling with delicate opened flowers to make the point. Tile: Edilgres Sirio. (left) Do not fear a mass infusion of stone. The designer of this luxurious bathroom created a magnificent ambience with stone styles from Italian mosaics to French limestone and marble. Interior Design: Nicholas Walker and Associates; Photo: Michael Garland.

ATMOSPHERE AND DRAMA

Simple, cool-colored tiles keep the flow in this bathroom, leading the eye to the garden outside the floor-to-ceiling windows. Copper accent tiles and matching accessories add interest. Interior Design: Scott Johnson; Photo: Tim Street-Porter.

Fire and Water

Year-round, people spend untold numbers of hours in their bathrooms and kitchens. These are the places where many are often at their most creative or where they rejuvenate their creative powers. Decorate these sanctuaries with murals or antique stone floors, or both, and they provide pleasing views and textural feedback. Nothing compares to the experience of walking barefoot across a stone floor! In this high-tech era, where the gray of a computer screen is too often the color of the day, we often crave the high-touch visuals that are the hallmark of the tile art form. Intricate handpainted tiles go back to the thirteenth century, when artisans decorated everything from palace entryways to baths. Stunning tilework enclosed stoves in the medieval period as well. This chapter features inspiring uses of tile, stone, and mosaics in kitchens, baths, living rooms, and at poolside. The collection shows the simple beauty of mono-chromatic rooms and those with bright, energizing palettes, in both simple and extravagant rooms.

(above) Complete a country theme by enhancing a stone fireplace with hand-crafted relief tiles of acorns, leaves, and wood. Tile: Pratt and Larson. **(left) Frost the cake of a dramatic kitchen with a wall of colorful antique tiles. This melange of intricately-patterned tiles pulls the overhanging hutch, the old-style stove, and the glass-paned cupboards together into a single graphic confection.** Tile: Beverly Ellsley; Photo: Phillip H. Ennis Photography.

Encircle a wood stove with tile rays of lemon yellow and warm up a sitting room on a cold winter's day. Continue terra-cotta floor tiles outside the door a few feet before laying brick—that way, on a sunny day, the room seems to merge with the glorious outdoors.

Interior Design: Barton Myers; Photo: Tim Street-Porter.

Use cobalt-blue tiles to create a tide of aquatic color. Here, a stately indoor pool is framed with a carpet of white stone and black diamond inlays. The gracious result is in keeping with the elegance of the surrounding architectural details. Photo: Roger Turk/Northlight Photography.

Give rein to interior design creativity on the hearth. Sequin broken tiles with color surprises or outline each with black to recall a stone cobwewb. Remember that the execution of ideas should be as solid as stone. Interior Design: Larry Totah; Photo: Tim Street-Porter.

(left) Complement a continuous wrap of windowpane squares with a checker-board of sand- and cream-colored tile that draws one poolside. Add a delicate blue band of tile to define a splash area and play off the blue and white tiles inside the pool. Design: Delight Nelson; Photo: Steve Vierra Photography. **(above) In a seaside room with floor to ceiling windows, avoid competition with the smashing view by adding a carpet of subdued silver-gray stone. Here, the interior squares match the driftwood color of the shoreline deck, which visually extends the room onto the beach.** Photo: Steve Vierra Photography.

(left and above) Make tile the star of a monochromatic bath-room. With one-color tile, basics like sinks, shelving, and faucets become important visuals, and their unique shapes, colors, and textures are emphasized. Design: Arthur de Mattos Casas.

(above and opposite) Contribute to the serene mood of an oceanside deck with satiny smooth Beaumaniere Classic French limestone set in squares, diamonds, triangles, and bars. With a view like this and a natural palette set by the sand and sea, a stone deck can afford to be self-effacing; it can become one with the horizon. Tile: Walker Zanger; Design: Randi Bernard, ASID; Photo: Stuart Watson.

(right) Who says a bathroom has to look like new? With tile that looks 100 years old, a bath with all the modern conveniences still feels like it's in an antique château. The worn edges, rich patina, and rustic color of Maison Française stone tiles give just that feeling. Tile: Walker Zanger; Design: Center Q Designs, Susan Whitman; Photo: Stuart Watson. **(below) Surround a luxurious, canopied soaking tub in buttery shades of marble tile to create a regal atmosphere. The tub is capped in more of the same, and the lip is more than wide enough to hold a candelabra for an evening bubble bath.** Interior Design: Anthony Catalfano; Photo: Steve Vierra Photography.

(opposite) **Exploit the vintage look of fireplace tiles finished with a handmade glaze in use since the 1930s; add a nautical touch with a tall ship motif in the corner relief tiles. Cerulean blue speaks to the colors of sea and sky that surround the light-filled living room of this Cape Cod vacation home.** Tile: Pewabic Tile; Design: Rosemary Porto Interiors; Photo: Stephen Sette-Ducati. **(left: above and below) Feature custom design work on both the interior and the deck surface of an indoor pool. The tumbled marble waves on these tiles are the product of a new technique of water-jet cutting. The pool basin is blue glass mosaic.** Design: Michael R. Golden.

Texture and Relief

The beauty of stone, its texture and bands of color, come from the forces of nature—the movement of the earth, vegetation, and animal life. Each stone, in essence, carries some history of the earth with it. When we walk across it, the distinctive sound reminds us of places we've traveled to, read, or dreamed about. Today, introducing stone into a home does exactly what it did hundreds of years ago. It presents an imperfect design component that adds a new level of architectural interest. It has the unique ability to make a room feel grand or casual, whether it covers a foyer wall or an entire kitchen floor.

Stone companies in the United States, England, Italy, and beyond continue to unearth exciting stone and slate for residential use. In Italy, for example, stone is very popular, and manufacturers are showing everything from rustic old stones to elegant and understated limestones. At Cersaie, the world's largest and most prestigious exhibition of ceramic tile and bathroom furnishings, authentic river pebbles recently were shown as decorations in field tiles, as intricate medallions, and in mesh-mounted borders. Relief tiles in modern and ancient patterns, as well as architectural ceramic tile designed for wainscoting, columns, moldings, and trims, were also shown. This chapter explores the uses of stone and tiles together with relief tiles in ceramic and glass. The design possibilities and combinations are endless.

(above) Tile: Waterworks. (right) Introduce an attractive texture with these classical sculptural motifs, which resemble the hand-carved wood that caps the wainscoting in grand old mansions. Here, the cocoa- and cream-colored wall tiles set at right angles add a level of visual interest to the wall. Tile: Walker Zanger; Photo: Stuart Watson.

(above) Add layering and detailing with ceramic relief tiles to give a bathroom a classic, rich feel. Notice how the single ribbon of high-gloss, black tiles accentuates the relief above and below, making the bone and mint-green tiles stand out. Tile: Walker Zanger; Photo: Stuart Watson. **(right) Anchor a large, pillared room with big, highly textured Lagos Azul limestone mixed with Pompei Rustic stone. The grand scale of the tiles stands up to the dramatic atmosphere of this formal room.** Stone: Walker Zanger; Interior Design: Michael Berman Design, Pasadena Showcase House of Design; Photo: Stuart Watson.

(opposite) Evoke the mystery of an archaeological find with rough-styled tiles that look recently unearthed. The curled tile edges and less-than-perfect fit and cuts give this bathroom a textured finish. Interior Design: Clodaugh Design International; Photo: Daniel Aubury. (left) Let small pattern details, such as these mosaic fish and stylized waves, enhance a bathroom floor. Tile: Paris Ceramics.

(**top right**) Design: Todd Graf, Ann Sacks Tile and Stone, Kohler, Wisconsin; Photo: Kohler Company. (**bottom right**) **Invoke a nature theme on one wall of a bathroom with these multi-toned relief tiles.** Tile : Ann Sacks Tile and Stone; Photo: Kohler Company. (**opposite**) **Consider a bath that is all about natural textures and tones. Here, loose stone climbs the wall in front of the tub to create a pleasant backdrop for natural light. It also works with the stone floor. Note how the tub tile carries the diamond shape from the floor, and the way the warm wood tones complement the stone.** Photo: Roger Turk/Northlight Photography.

TEXTURE AND RELIEF

(below) Tile: Walker Zanger; Photo: Stuart Watson. **(right) Lower the temperature in a hot Houston bathroom with cool blue-green tiles and accents in pewter. The elegant sink, plumbing fixtures, and mirror are all pewter. The irregular colors, tile to tile, come from double-firing the tiles and adding several glazes.** Tile: ICT, Inc.; Tile Design: Talavera de Mexico; Interior Design: Susan Baker; Photo: Jack Thompson.

TEXTURE AND RELIEF

(left) Generate the look of an authentic country farmhouse kitchen by framing soft blond wood with Tuscany stone pavers and borders. Choose a Botticino farmhouse sink and frame it in stone to continue the casual theme. Utilize wall space and create a decorative stone shelf. Tile: Walker Zanger.

(above) Evoke a rustic country farmhouse in a kitchen work area with a wall of imperfectly cut stone. Here, the stone expanse is sequined with a relief border of grapes and a single leaf. The line of the border parallels that of the overhead rack hung with utensils of unusual shapes. Tile: Vic Samaritoni, Ann Sacks Tile and Stone; Photo: Kohler Company.

Rough-cut stone resembles an outdoor pathway and, with dramatic contrast, emphasizes the simple, sleek lines of the cabinets and countertop. Design: Dalia Kitchen Design, Inc.; Cabinets: Alno, Germany.

(above) Tile: Artistic Tile. **(left) Surround a sunken whirlpool bath with stone to make it the focal point of an indoor spa. The stone's natural imperfections and color gradations add interest of their own.** Interior Design: Andrew Baty; Photo: Tim Street-Porter.

Mixed Media

As far back as the twelfth century, imaginative craftspeople spun tile, stone, and mosaics together in floor and wall tiles, and even pavement. Complex, brilliantly-colored geometric shapes, letters, and scenes on tile were set amid stone or bricks, making public places studies in art. Today, tile artists, manufacturers, and fashion designers are showing new, exciting mixed-media combinations—in single tiles and in patterns—tile to tile. For example, octagonal-cut stone tiles are centered with buttons of black marble or bordered in tiny mosaics. Walls of iridescent glass mosaic are accented by a band of flat stone. Mixing and matching are not subject to rules—creativity is the force that knows no limit.

At Cersaie, the world-renowned tile exhibition held in Bologna, some Italian manufacturers experiment with mixing glass, metal, and enamel to create unusual glazes and surface treatments. Others incorporate touches of aluminum, copper, and gold to create surface variations. Glass appears on large-format tiles and tiny mosaics feature new, brilliant colors. This chapter on mixed media shows examples of these new materials, thus illustrating how creative the mixing of tile, stone, glass, and mosaic on the same or neighboring surfaces can be.

Surround an oversized sink, which is lined with mosaic stone, with a garden of relief tiles. Continue the theme throughout the kitchen; in this craftsman bungalow, more relief tiles crown the cooking area. Notice the decorative grape border and the stone and mosaic floor. Tile: Pratt and Larson; Photo: Jon Jensen.

(above) Finish a bathroom with Citrus Gold, a line of antique tiles that range in color from mustard to deep curry. Use tile shards to form wall frames. For the floor, set deep orange bricks at contrasting angles. The colorful sink shown here is of Talavera ceramic with brass fittings, both made in Mexico. Tile: ICT, Inc.; Tile Design: Talavera de Mexico; Interior Design: Susan Baker; Photo: Jack Thompson. (right) Consider mixing Italian marble textures and colors in the bath. Here, a marble composite rug with shiny metal flecks and deep coral and gray borders conveys a look of distinction. Notice how the sea of white tiles is broken up with bright buttons of marble and how the designer capped the wall in a band of coral marble. Interior Design: Richard L. Schlesinger Interiors; Photo: Oleg March.

Conjure an atmosphere of fantasy in a bath that takes the term mixed media to the max. Use soft colors that let the eyes take in the myriad details with ease, from the robin's-egg-blue mosaics that line the tub, to the pastel flower tile bands and textured sink treatments. **Tile: Pratt and Larson; Photo: Jon Jensen.**

(left) Bring a glow of warmth to a bathroom with burnt-
orange, terra-cotta tiles in a mix of uniform squares and tiny
mosaics. A continuous band of diamond-shaped, royal-blue
and black mosaic tiles adds a splash of color. Tile: Oceanside
Glasstile, Inc./Tiles, A Refined Selection. **(above) Inset a custom
mosaic pattern from the Tessera line of tile to add color and
new dimension to a gray-hued stone floor. The rainbow
colored tiles elicit a suggestion of the same shades from the
dull stone.** Tile: Oceanside Glasstile, Inc./Tiles, A Refined Selection.

(opposite) Add the fantastic to the functional in a bath area designed for contemplation. This breathtaking room, decorated in a mix of decorative mosaic tiles and a big, dreamy mural, is a perfect place to reflect on the possibilities of the future. Design: Michael R. Golden Design; Photo: Noah Greenberg.

(left) Combine tile with mosaics in a deep, luxurious whirlpool bath and create a beautiful place, whether full of warm bathwater or not. This exquisite bath design demonstrates that creative energy need not always focus on floors and walls. Tile: Pratt and Larson; Photo: Stephen Cridland.

(above) Sometimes simplicity makes the mood. One tile style, in one color, creates a serene bath. Design: Arthur de Mattas Casas. (opposite) Raise the visual interest in a room by placing stone borders alongside delicate mosaic tiles. Because of the complementary color palette, the rugged texture of the stone around this shower emphasizes the more controlled regularity of the interior tilework. Interior Design: Rob Quigley; Photo: Tim Street-Porter.

Directory

TILE DESIGNERS

Absolute Kitchen & Bath
Mitch Chester
69 Glen Cove Road
Greenvale, NY 11548
(516) 621-6500
Photography: Oleg March

Blakeley-Bazely Ltd.
3463 State Street, Suite 131
Santa Barbara, CA 93105
(805) 965-1272 or (323) 653-3548

Erika Brunson Design Associates (EBDA)
903 West Bourne Drive
Los Angeles, CA 90069
(310) 652-1970

Clodagh Design, International
670 Broadway
New York, NY 10012
(212) 780-5300
Photography: Daniel Aubry

Arthur de Mattos Casas
Studio Arthur de Mattos Casas
Alameda Ministro Rocha Azevedo 1052
Sao Paulo, Brazil
CEP 01410002
011-55-11-282-6311
Photography: Tuca Rein

Dalia Kitchen Design, Inc.
One Design Center Place, #643
Boston, MA 02210
(617) 482-2566

Mark Enos
Enos & Co.
705 North Alfred Street
Los Angeles, CA 90069
(323) 655-0109

Garden Design Magazine
Meigher Communications
100 Avenue of the Americas, 7th Floor
New York, NY 10013
(212) 219-7454
Design: Ann Powell
Photography: Andre Baranowski

Michael R. Golden Design
37 West 20th Street
New York, NY 10001
(212) 645-3001

Gloria Kosco & Mimi Strang
Decoratta Ornamental Terra Cotta
115 East Main Street
Silverdale, PA 18962
(215) 453-8601

M.E. Tile Co.
400 East Sibley Road
P. O. Box 1595
Harvey, IL 60426
(708) 210-3229

Todd Oldham
The Hotel
801 Collins Avenue
Miami Beach, FL 33139
(305) 531-4411
Photography: Todd Eberle

Sunny Days Flooring
Robert Cesar, Design Consultant
2317 West Ridgeway
Cedar Falls, IA 50613
(319) 231-4849

Tile by Design
Nan Owen
24291 Sunnybrook Circle
Lake Forest, CA 92630
(949) 855-7877
Photography: Leonard Myszynski, David Glomb

Nicholas Walker and Associates
1011 North Orange Drive
Los Angeles, CA 90038
(323) 874-5588
Photography: Michael Garland

Sara Zook Designs Ltd.
2001 Youngfeild Street
Golden, CO 80401
(303) 237-4544\tab

TILE MANUFACTURERS

Italian Tile

Italian Trade Commission
499 Park Avenue
New York, NY 10022
(212) 980-1500

Bardelli,through Hastings Tile (212) 674-9700
Cerasarda, through Ex, Inc. (212-758-2593
Il Pavone, through Artistic Tile (212) 727-9331

Spanish Tile

ASCER (Spanish Ceramic Tile Manufacturers Association)
Camino Caminas
12003 Castellon
Spain
34 64 72 7200

Trade Commission of Spain
2655 Le Jeune Road, Suite 114
Coral Gables, FL 33134
(305) 446-4387

Ann Sacks Tile and Stone
8120 N.E. 33rd Drive
Portland, OR 97211
(503) 280-9701

Artistic Tile, Inc.
339 Princeton-Hightstown Road
Cranbury, NJ 08512
(609) 490-0999

Bisazza
8530 North West 30th Terrace
Miami, FL 33122
(305) 597-4090

Bisazza, North American Showroom
12 West 24th Street, 24th floor
New York, New York 10010
(212) 463-0620

Country Floors/WC Tile Guide
Eric R. Carlson
8735 Melrose Avenue
Los Angeles, CA 90069
(310) 657-0570

Edilgres Sirio
Via Circondariale San Francesco 122
41402 Fiorano
Modena
Italy